WHAT IS A PANDEMIC?

By Kara L. Laughlin

The
Child's
World®
childsworld.com

Published by The Child's World®
1980 Lookout Drive
Mankato, MN 56003-1705
800-599-READ
www.childsworld.com

Photos ©: abolukbas/Shutterstock.
com: 6; DigitalMammoth/
Shutterstock.com: cover, 2;
frank60/Shutterstock.com: 13;
Jeka/Shutterstock.com: 5; Josse
Lieferinxe/Public domain: 8;
JPC-PROD/Shutterstock.com: 17;
Kate Krav-Rude/Shutterstock.com:
22; leungchopan/Shutterstock.
com: 11; Suzanne Tucker/
Shutterstock.com: 14; Unknown
author/Public domain: 18

ISBN 9781503853164
(Reinforced Library Binding)

ISBN 9781503853225
(Portable Document Format)

ISBN 9781503853287
(Online Multi-user eBook)

LCCN: 2020939119

Printed in the United
States of America

About the Author
Kara Laughlin lives in
Leesburg, VA with her
husband, three kids, and
a dog. She has written
over 50 nonfiction books
for children.

CONTENTS

CHAPTER ONE

What Is a Pandemic?

Do you remember your last cold? How did it start? Itchy throat? Stuffy nose? Maybe you weren't even sure you were sick. But soon everything changed. What started small quickly made your whole body sick.

In the same way, a new **virus** can start in one place and quickly make the whole world sick. It becomes a **pandemic**.

Some people with colds get very sick. Other people don't feel sick at all.

An outbreak of a new virus called the "new coronavirus" began in China in 2019. Despite efforts such as cleaning and using masks, the virus quickly became a pandemic.

Viruses are always making someone sick. Usually, that's no big deal. People get sick. They get better. The number of sick people stays about the same.

Sometimes a virus causes an **outbreak**. An outbreak happens when more and more people get sick. Some outbreaks flare up and die down. Some outbreaks spread. An outbreak that spreads through a large area is an **epidemic**. An epidemic that spreads through the world is a pandemic.

COVID-19 FACT

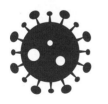

The COVID-19 pandemic is caused by a virus nicknamed the "new coronavirus." It's full name is SARS-CoV-2. It causes a disease called COVID-19.

Without proper medicines and cleanliness, the Black Death caused millions of deaths. Scientists finally discovered the pandemic was caused by a bacteria carried by fleas.

CHAPTER TWO

Pandemics through Time

Pandemics have been around for a long time. They spread when people travel throughout the world. One of the worst pandemics was the Black Death. Traders in the mid-1300s brought spices from Asia to Europe. They also brought **bacteria** that carried the Black Death to Europe and other areas.

COVID-19 FACT

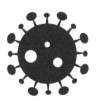

The first pandemic on record began in Athens, Greece in 430 B.C. Scientists today think it was a disease called typhoid fever.

Today's world is more connected than ever. People fly across oceans every day. Their germs fly with them. In the last 40 years, many new viruses have spread across the world. AIDS, Ebola, SARS, and H1N1 flu have all caused pandemics. COVID-19 is a new pandemic. It appeared in China in late 2019. It took just three months to spread over the globe.

COVID-19 FACT

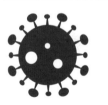

Different viruses spread in different ways. The new coronavirus that causes COVID-19 spreads through droplets when people talk, cough, or sneeze.

Germs can spread easily on airplanes as well as other public modes of transportation.

CHAPTER THREE

How Pandemics Spread

How do pandemics spread so fast? Often it's because they are new. After people fight off a virus, they are **immune** for a time. That means they can't catch it again. When many people are immune to a virus, it can't spread well. Immune people can't catch it. Others don't catch it because there are so few people to catch it from!

A new virus is different. Nobody is immune. It can **infect** anyone, and that lets it spread fast.

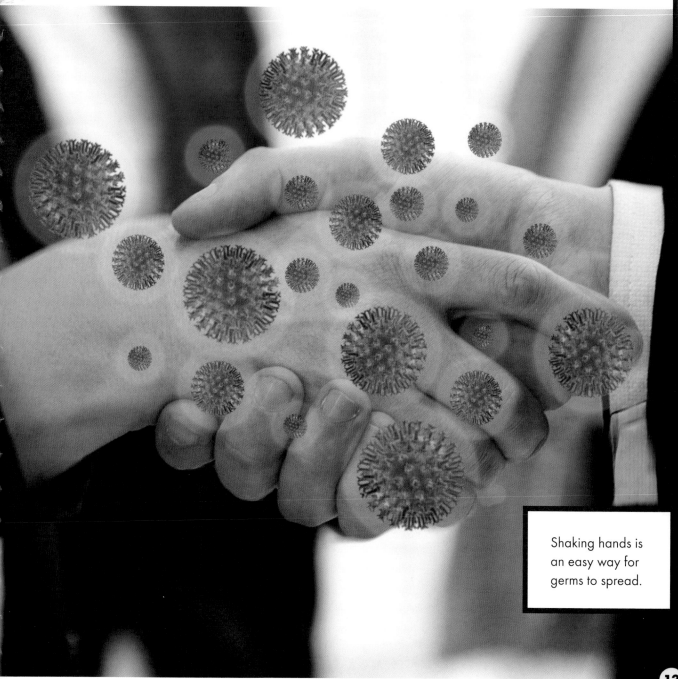

Shaking hands is
an easy way for
germs to spread.

People who have been around someone with COVID-19 have been exposed to the disease. They should quarantine themselves for at least 14 days after the exposure.

CHAPTER FOUR

Fighting Pandemics

The first step in fighting a new virus is to stop its spread. Sick people stay where they won't get others sick. Health workers find people who could have been exposed to the virus. Those people may go into **quarantine**. They also stay away from others for a time. If they stay well long enough, they know they won't spread the virus.

COVID-19 FACT

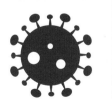

During the Black Death, sailors coming to Venice had to stay on their ships for forty days. "Quarantine" comes from the Italian word for forty: *quarantino*.

With time, we can find drugs to fight pandemics. When people first started getting sick with a virus called HIV, many of them died of AIDS. Today drugs help people with HIV stay healthy.

Vaccines fight pandemics too. Vaccines are dead viruses or pieces of virus that doctors put in our bodies (usually with a needle). Vaccines wake up a body's germ-fighters. The germ-fighters make us immune without making us sick. Measles and mumps are viruses we prevent with vaccines.

COVID-19 FACT

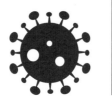

The United States suffered a polio epidemic from 1916 to the 1960s. It ended when Dr. Jonas Salk introduced a vaccine that was used across the country.

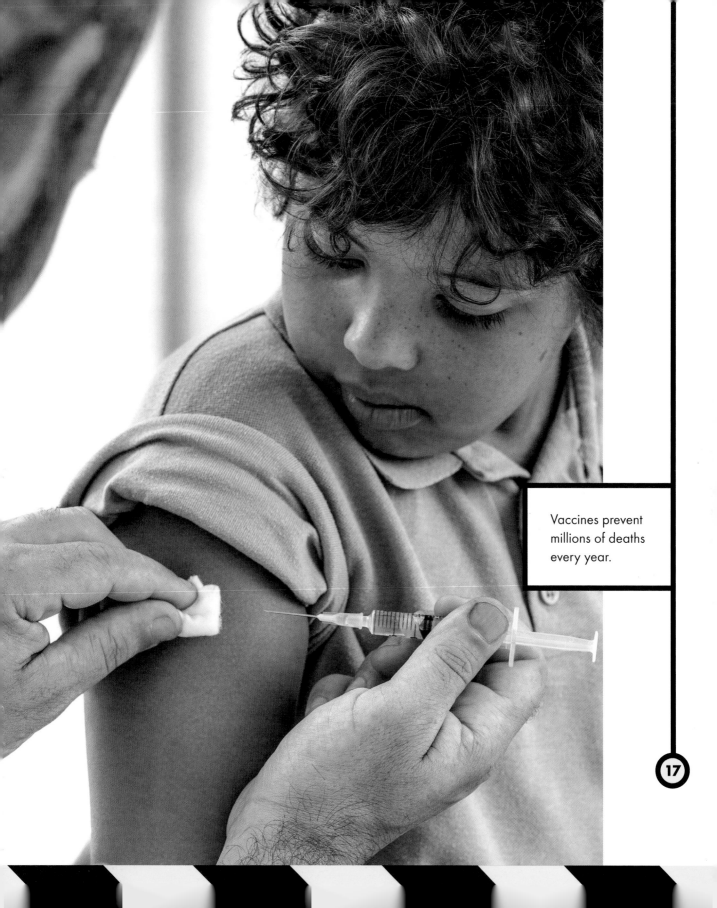

Vaccines prevent
millions of deaths
every year.

This photo shows people in San Francisco wearing masks during the flu pandemic of 1918.

Sometimes pandemics help us to fight them. Viruses are always changing. Sometimes they become less dangerous. An H1N1 flu virus caused a bad flu pandemic in 1918. H1N1 has changed many times. The changes seem to be making it less deadly.

COVID-19 FACT

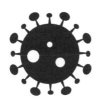

During the 1918 flu pandemic, approximately 500 million people became infected with the virus.

There are ways you can fight pandemics, too. When you feel sick, stay home. Keep your hands clean. Cough or sneeze into your elbow. Wear a mask when you go out.

Every day, people fight pandemics. Some find vaccines. Some make new drugs. Some find cures. Maybe one day you will join them!

COVID-19 FACT

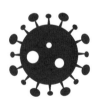

Washing your hands for 20 seconds or longer kills the new coronavirus and can help stop the spread of COVID-19.

THINK ABOUT IT

Here are some ways to learn more about pandemics and how diseases spread.

See the Spread. Try this to see how a virus can spread. Rub a teaspoon of flour between your palms, then do some of the things you do every day. Drink a glass of water. Give someone a hug. Read a book. Did all the flour stay on your hands? Did any get on your face? What activity spread the most flour?

Stop the Spread. Imagine you are a doctor with a new virus in your community. What are three things you would do to prevent a pandemic? What would you do first? Second? Third? Why?

Design a Well Room. Do you have friends you can't visit right now? It's hard to stay apart during a pandemic. Draw a room that helps people be together without spreading germs. Show it to someone in your family or mail it to someone you wish you could visit.

It can be hard to understand how staying at home slows the spread of a virus. Programmers Joseph Davies and Hugo Barne are fans of Minecraft. They created a way for kids to see how quarantines affect the spread of a disease. Blockdown is a free Minecraft map. Players manage an imagined outbreak. They can watch what happens or play as a nurse. Players control the outbreak from a tower. A hospital in the basement houses zombies until they are cured.